T0055969

The Wind in the Willows

an entertainment
based on the book by
Kenneth Grahame

Words by David Grant
Music by John Rutter

Kenneth Grahame's enchanting book *The Wind in the Willows* was first published in 1908 and has remained one of the best-loved of children's classics, enjoyed equally by generations of adult readers too. This musical adaptation was originally written as an 'entertainment' for The King's Singers (six male voices) and the City of London Sinfonia to perform at a family concert. The present published version, for five soloists, narrator and chorus, can either be performed as a concert piece or staged in various ways. Children can participate in the chorus (and as field-mice), though some altos, tenors and basses are essential. The main roles are intended for adult or teenage singers; Mole, a part originally written for male alto, could alternatively be sung by a boy alto, boy soprano, or baritone. The orchestral accompaniment is within the capacity of good teenage or amateur players; in the absence of orchestra, piano accompaniment would be adequate, with double-bass and drums if possible.

Music Department
OXFORD UNIVERSITY PRESS

for the King's Singers

THE WIND IN THE WILLOWS

Words by
DAVID GRANT

Music by
JOHN RUTTER

1: PROLOGUE

(Chorus)

© Oxford University Press 1986

Printed in Great Britain
OXFORD UNIVERSITY PRESS, MUSIC DEPARTMENT, GREAT CLARENDON STREET, OXFORD, OX2 6DP

Photocopying this copyright material is ILLEGAL.

8
poco a poco cresc.
(n)
mp
lis - ten,
poco a poco cresc.
p cresc.
lis - ten
(n)
poco a poco cresc.
cresc.
(n)
lis - ten
(n)
(n)
poco a poco cresc.
Lis - ten
(n)
(n)
poco a poco cresc.
Ped.
12
mp cresc.
lis - ten, lis - ten, lis - ten:
cresc.
(n)
lis - ten, lis - ten:
mp cresc.
(n)
mp cresc.
(n)
mp cresc.
(n)
cresc. sempre

A
15
S.
mf dolce
unis.
A.
Lis - ten to the sound of the wind in the
T.
unis.
B.
mf dolce
A
Ww.
mf legato
Ped.
Ped.
Ped.
18
mp
wil - lows Whis-per-ing through the branch - es and the
mp
mp
21
B
leaves. Come a - way and lis - ten
Fl.
B
Ped.

24
to a sto - ry of long a - go and far a - way; When the ri - ver
pp
dim.
28
mur - mured its ma - gi - cal mu - sic to the scent - ed breeze.
p
32
poco rit.
C a tempo
Lis - ten to the e - cho of
cresc.
Vlns.

35
S.
soft dis - tant voi - ces call - ing us,
A.
soft dis - tant voi - ces call - ing us,
T.
soft dis - tant voi - ces call - ing us,
B.
soft dis - tant voi - ces call - ing us,
Fl.
Ped.
38
p
cresc.
call - ing us a - way,
p
cresc.
mp
cresc.
call - ing us a - way, a - way,
p
cresc.
mp
cresc.
call - ing us a - way, a - way, a - way,
p
cresc.
mp
call - ing us a - way, a - way,
Ob.
p
cresc.
mp cresc.

41
mf
f
mp
dim.
p
call - ing us, call - ing us a - way, a - way, a -
mf
f
mf dim.
mp dim.
call - ing us, call - ing us a - way, a - way, a - way,
mf
f
dim.
p
call - ing us, call - ing us a - way, a - way, a -
f
mf dim.
p
call - ing us a - way, a - way, a -
mf cresc.
f
dim.
mp dim.
Ped.
Ped.
Ped.
D
45
p
dim.
rit.
pp
- way, a - way, a - way.
p
dim.
pp
a - way.
dim.
pp
- way, a - way.
dim.
pp
- way, a - way.
D
rit.
p
dim.
pp
Ped.

2: NARRATION

NARRATOR:

'Hang spring cleaning!' said Mole, flinging down his whitewash brush. 'Bother and blow!' said Mole, and he bolted out of the house, without even waiting to put on his coat. Something up above was calling him into the sunlight and away . . . across the meadows and alongside the copses . . . trotting along the river bank where, all of a sudden, he sat down, entranced and bewitched.

As he sat on the grass and looked across the river, he became aware of a bright little star winking at him from the opposite bank. The star became an eye . . . and then there was another eye . . . then a small brown face . . . with whiskers . . . (*Attacca No. 3*)

3: RIVER SCENE AND SONG

(Rat, Mole, and Chorus)

10
MOLE
rit.
RAT
f
Would you like to come?
Well. . .
I'm not sure. . .
O
Ob.
p
Fl.
Ped.
Ped.
14
a tempo
p
A
Fast; strict time (♩=176)
cresc.
come on, old chap—
Just
step in-to the boat;
Now you
mp
17
poco a poco
mf
real-ly are a-float!
Put the pic-nic ham-per un-der your seat,— sit
cresc.

21
CHORUS S. mf lightly
A.
Doo doo doo doo doo
T.
B. mf lightly
(RAT)
back, re - lax, there'll be plen - ty to eat!
f
24
B
doo
mf
Me O my!
mf
mf brightly
B
A life on the ri - ver,
Yes, a
Cymbal
mf

27
My O me!
O
p
life on the ri - ver,
Why, a life on the ri - ver,
30
my, O me,
Oo
mf
That's the life to set my heart all a - qui - ver!
With the

33
Splish, splosh, bzz bzz
splash-ing of the oars, and the buzz-ing of the bees. Now I
37
Me O my! My O me!
ask, did you ev-er See a hap-pi-er fel-la Than a

41
gliss.
Hey ho!
mp
Rap - ture!
gliss.
mp
fel-la who's a-float
In his lit-tle wood-en boat?
Cymbal
p
C
(RAT and MOLE with CHORUS)
45
unis.
p
Cu-cum-ber sand-wich-es, sa - vou - ry re - lish, Pa - té with truf-fles and cran-ber-ry jel - ly,
unis.
p
C
p

47
Ham and tongue and beef and goose-ber - ry pie: O my!
49
unis.
poco cresc.
Mus - tard and cress and Rus - sian sa - lad, Ban - bu - ry cake and su - ga - ry dough - nuts,
unis.
poco cresc.
51
mf
Bran - dy snaps and fudge and bot - tles of squash: O gosh!
mf
Vc.

53
(S.)
Hard - boiled eggs,
Peach-es and cream,
(A.)
Le-mon me-ringue,
(T.)
A - pri - cot flan,
(B.)
55
unis. mf cresc.
Cut up in con-ven - i - ent lit - tle wedge shapes:
Ve - ni - son pas - ty with wal-nuts and grapes,
unis.
cresc.
cresc.
57
f
D
mp lightly
just so!
Pit - a - pat!
f
mp lightly
MOLE f
My
D
heart's all a - shi - ver;
It feels all a - shi - ver;
f
mp
(+ Str. sust.)

61
Pat - a - pit!
Oo
My heart's all a - shi - ver
Just to be in a boat on the ri - ver,
65
mf
p
float - ing down the stream,
Oo
mf
p
With the sigh - ing of the breeze
And the bir - dies in the trees.
p

69
E
f
mf
Quack quack!
In your life
MOLE
Now I ask, did you ev - er
See two hap- pi - er fel - las
RAT
Now I ask, did you ev- er
See two hap- pi - er fel - las
E
73
bliss - ful!
Hey ho!
Than Rat and Mole a - float
Hey ho!
In their
Than Rat and Mole a - float
Hey ho!
In their

4: NARRATION

NARRATOR:

And so the two contented animals made their way slowly up the river to Rat's house. Rat spent the summer and the autumm showing Mole the sights of the River Bank, and introducing him to all his friends . . . except for one . . . the rather grumpy Mr Badger, who lived in the Wild Wood.

'Couldn't you invite him to dinner?' asked Mole.

'He wouldn't come,' said Rat. 'Simply hates Society.'

'Well then, why don't we go and call on him?' suggested Mole.

'It's a long journey,' replied Rat. 'But perhaps we *should* pay him a visit, especially as Christmas is coming on.'

So one cold December day they set off together through the Wild Wood, rather thoughtfully . . .

Alternative version of final sentence (*to be used if No. 5 is omitted*): So one cold December day they set off together through the Wild Wood, till they reached Badger's house.

* 5: THE JOURNEY TO BADGER'S HOUSE
(The Wild Wood Carol)

(Rat and Chorus)

(Words by J. R.)

* This number may be omitted if it is desired to shorten the work.

A
12
2. A wea - ry jour - ney one win - ter's night: No hope of shel - ter, no rest in
CHORUS
S. p
A.
(Hum)
T.
B. p
A
pp
16
mp
p
sight. Who was the crea - ture that bore Ma - ry? A sim - ple don - key.
mp
p
mp
p
Vlns.
mp espress.

22
B
20
p
3. And when they came in - to Beth - lem
B
p
pp
24
mp
mf
Town They found a sta - ble to lay them down; For their com - pa - nions that Christ-mas
mp
mf
28
Night, An ox and an ass.
mp
C
Night, (Hum)
mp
C
Ob.
mp
mf

33
unis. mf
4. And then an an - gel came down to earth To bear the
unis.
mf
Hp.
mf
f
37
stringendo f
news of the Sa - viour's birth; The first to mar - vel were shep - herds
f
stringendo
f
40
rall.
Tempo I
And sheep with their lambs.
mp
poor,
(Hum)
mp
rall.
Tempo I
Ob.
mp
dim.
p dim.

24
D
45
RAT
p
Sing O the wild wood, the green hol - ly; The si - lent ri - ver and bar - ren
pp
(Hum)
D
pp
Vlns.
pp
49
mp
rit.
dim.
p
tree; The hum - ble crea - tures that no man sees: Sing
cresc.
p
dim.
cresc.
p
dim.
rit.
52
a tempo
O the wild wood.
a tempo
Str.
Ob.
pp

6: AT BADGER'S HOUSE

(Mole, Rat, Badger, and Field-Mice)

10
ca - rol - sing - ing a - gain . . . Come in, come in, and sit by the
13
(knock at the door)
A
(♩. = ♩ of preceding)
FIELD-MICE
f sour, nasty tone
fire.
We wish you a mer-ry Christ-mas, we
Str. pizz.
f
16
wish you a mer - ry Christ - mas, we wish you a mer - ry Christ - mas, we
18
wish you a mer - ry Christ - mas . . .
BADGER f
mf
O con - found you, wretch - ed field - mice! I sup -
mf

21
FIELD-MICE
(♩=♩. of preceding)
Oh thank you, Mis - ter Bad - ger, sir,
BADGER
- pose you'd bet - ter come in.
(♩=♩. of preceding)
24
thank you!
You may la - ter sing one verse of some brief sooth - ing
p
28
ca - rol . . . for the mo - ment be si - lent while I talk with Mis - ter Rat and Mis - ter
rit.

B a tempo (♩=80)
32
Mole. Now tell me, dear Rat: What is the news of the out - side
tranquillo
35
world? And in par-ti-cu-lar, what of our reck-less young friend Toad?
Vivace (♩=132)
38
RAT
mf
There's no-thing new a-bout the
f
dim.
p
con Ped. sempre
40
Toad ex-cept his la-test cra-zes.
BADGER
mf
A-lack! a

42
There is no end to what he'll
prey to fool - ish cra - zes . . .
44
find; His sta - mi - na a - ma - zes.
MOLE
mf
I
BADGER
A - ma - zes?
D
46
blame his pa - rents— such well - in - ten - tioned folk—
But
stacc. simile

48
then, a - las, they spoiled him.
FIELD-MICE
f
Our
BADGER
I fear they must have spoiled him.
50
aun - tie says 'E tried to knock the vil - lage p'lice - man's
mf
52
hel - met off, But then they foiled 'im!
RAT
mf
3
It's a
BADGER
f
mf
3
Be si - lent! It's a

54
MOLE
It's a
prob - lem, it's a prob - lem, it's a ter - ri - ble, ter - ri - ble prob - lem! It's a
prob - lem, it's a prob - lem, it's a ter - ri - ble, ter - ri - ble prob - lem! It's a
56
prob - lem, it's a prob - lem, What a ter - ri - ble, ter - ri - ble prob - lem!
prob - lem, it's a prob - lem, What a ter - ri - ble, ter - ri - ble prob - lem!
prob - lem, it's a prob - lem, What a ter - ri - ble, ter - ri - ble prob - lem!
E (MOLE, RAT,
58 and BADGER)
We'll have to do some - thing a - bout Mis - ter Toad, His
p più legato

60
con - duct is tru - ly ap - pal - ling. He's fool - ish and fi - ckle and ea - si - ly led, Con -
62
cresc.
- cei - ted and boast - ful and weak in the head, He'll go to the bad and then soon he'll be dead:
cresc.
64
f
What can we do to pre-vent him from fall - ing?
RAT
mf
Last
f
mf
dim.
mp
F
66
month he bought a gip - sy ca - ra - van In bright ca - na - ry

68
yel - low.
The
BADGER
mf
Oh no! not bright ca - na - ry yel - low!
70
co - lour's sure - ly bad e - nough, But worse was still to
72
MOLE
mf
I think that Ox - ford
RAT
fol - low.
BADGER
A - lack!
p

* English sugar-coated confections

80
MOLE
It's a
prob - lem, it's a prob - lem, It's a ter - ri - ble, ter - ri - ble prob - lem! It's a
prob - lem, it's a prob - lem, It's a ter - ri - ble, ter - ri - ble prob - lem! It's a
82
prob - lem, it's a prob - lem, What a ter - ri - ble, ter - ri - ble prob - lem!
prob - lem, it's a prob - lem, What a ter - ri - ble, ter - ri - ble prob - lem!
prob - lem, it's a prob - lem, What a ter - ri - ble, ter - ri - ble prob - lem!
84
MOLE, RAT, and BADGER
G
pp sotto voce
We'll have to do some - thing a - bout Mis - ter Toad, His

86
con - duct is tru - ly ap - pal - ling. He's fool - ish and fi - ckle and ea - si - ly led, Con -
88
cresc.
- cei - ted and boast - ful and weak in the head, He'll go to the bad and then soon he'll be dead:
cresc.
90
f
What can we do to pre - vent him from fall - ing?
f
p
mf
H
RAT
92
f
This month, I think you must have heard: It's mo - tor cars and
marc. sempre

(MOLE and BADGER gasp)
94
awestruck
speed - ing . . . At more than twen - ty miles an hour! His
96
reck - less fol - ly as he drives To tra - ge - dy is
98
MOLE
lead - ing. The coun - try - side is
BADGER
How true!
p
f
100
FIELD-MICE
f
Our
MOLE
now no lon - ger safe; His mo - tor - ing's a me - nace!
p

102
FIELD-MICE
grand - ma says . . .
MOLE mf
We'll
BADGER
f
Shush!
RAT and BADGER mf
We'll
f
mp
I
FIELD-MICE
104
f (nasty tone still!)
Good King Wen - ces - las looked out
(RAT, MOLE, and BADGER)
have to do some-thing a-bout Mis-ter Toad, His con - duct is tru - ly ap-pal - ling. He's
Vln.
pizz.
mf
etc.
106
On the Feast of Ste - phen.
foo - lish and fi - ckle and ea - si - ly led, Con - cei - ted and boast - ful and weak in the head, He'll

108
FIELD-MICE
Bright - ly shone the moon that night . . . The
MOLE
go to the bad and then soon he'll be dead:
RAT
go to the bad and then soon he'll be dead:
What shall we do?
BADGER
go to the bad and then soon he'll be dead:
What shall we do?
110
first
Now - ell the an - gel did
What shall we do?
What shall we do?
What shall we do?
What shall we
What shall we do?
mp
cresc.

112
accel.
J Più vivace (♩. = 144)
say . . .
ff
mf
What shall we do? We'll sort him out, we'll put him right, We'll
do?
What shall we do? We'll sort him out, we'll put him right, We'll
What shall we do? We'll sort him out, we'll put him right, We'll
accel.
Più vivace (♩. = 144)
114 MOLE, RAT, and BADGER
cresc.
set him straight, we'll lec - ture him, We'll get him on the rails And bash him
cresc.
116 FIELD-MICE
f
On the first day of Christ - mas my
up if all else fails, Yes that's what we'll do
f dim.

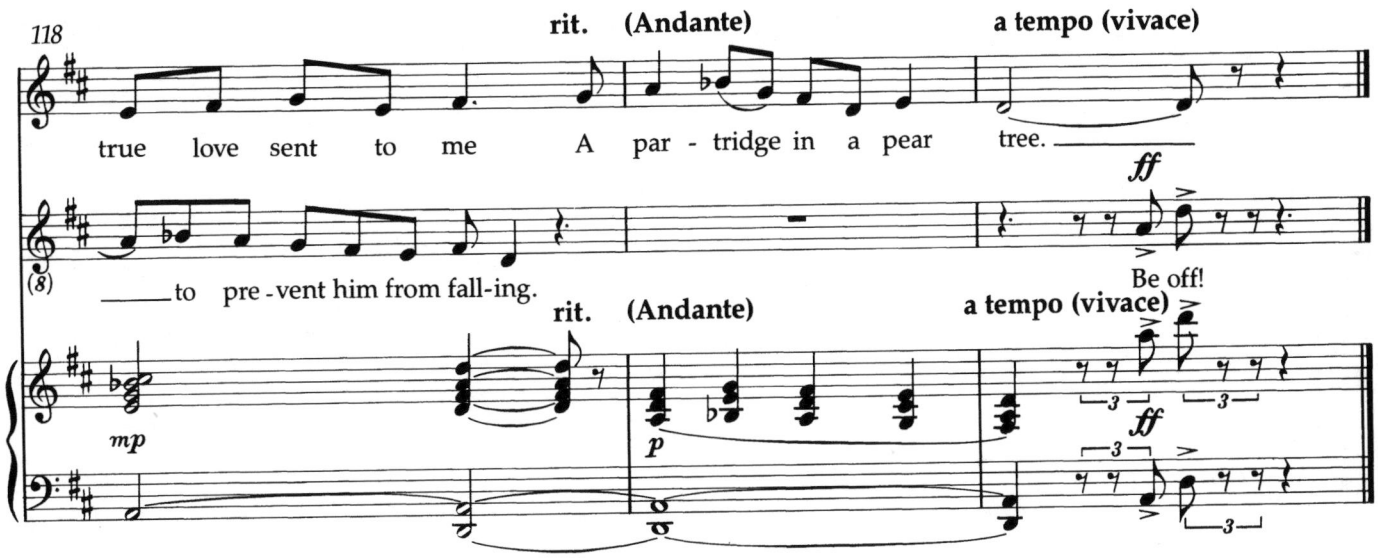

NARRATOR:

And that's how things were left. Rat and Mole returned home the next day, determined to save Toad from the dreadful consequences of his new motor car craze. The rest of the winter passed quietly, but one morning, quite early in the spring, all three animals happened to be standing in a peaceful lane near the river bank when they heard a most terrible commotion in the distance . . . (*End of narration to overlap with start of No. 7*)

7: TOAD'S CAR

(Chorus)

Note to conductor: What follows represents Toad's car (1908 vintage) already going fast as it becomes audible in the distance, getting nearer, slowing down and stopping. Allocate voices in whatever way works best.

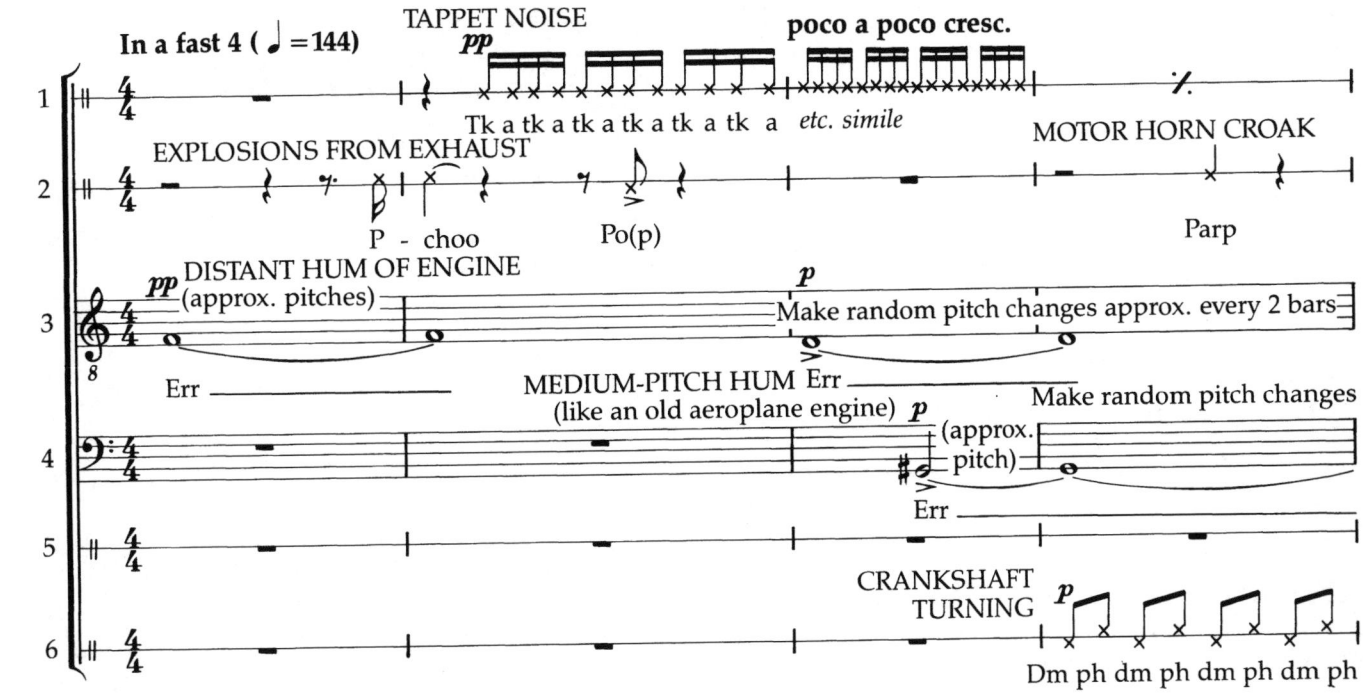

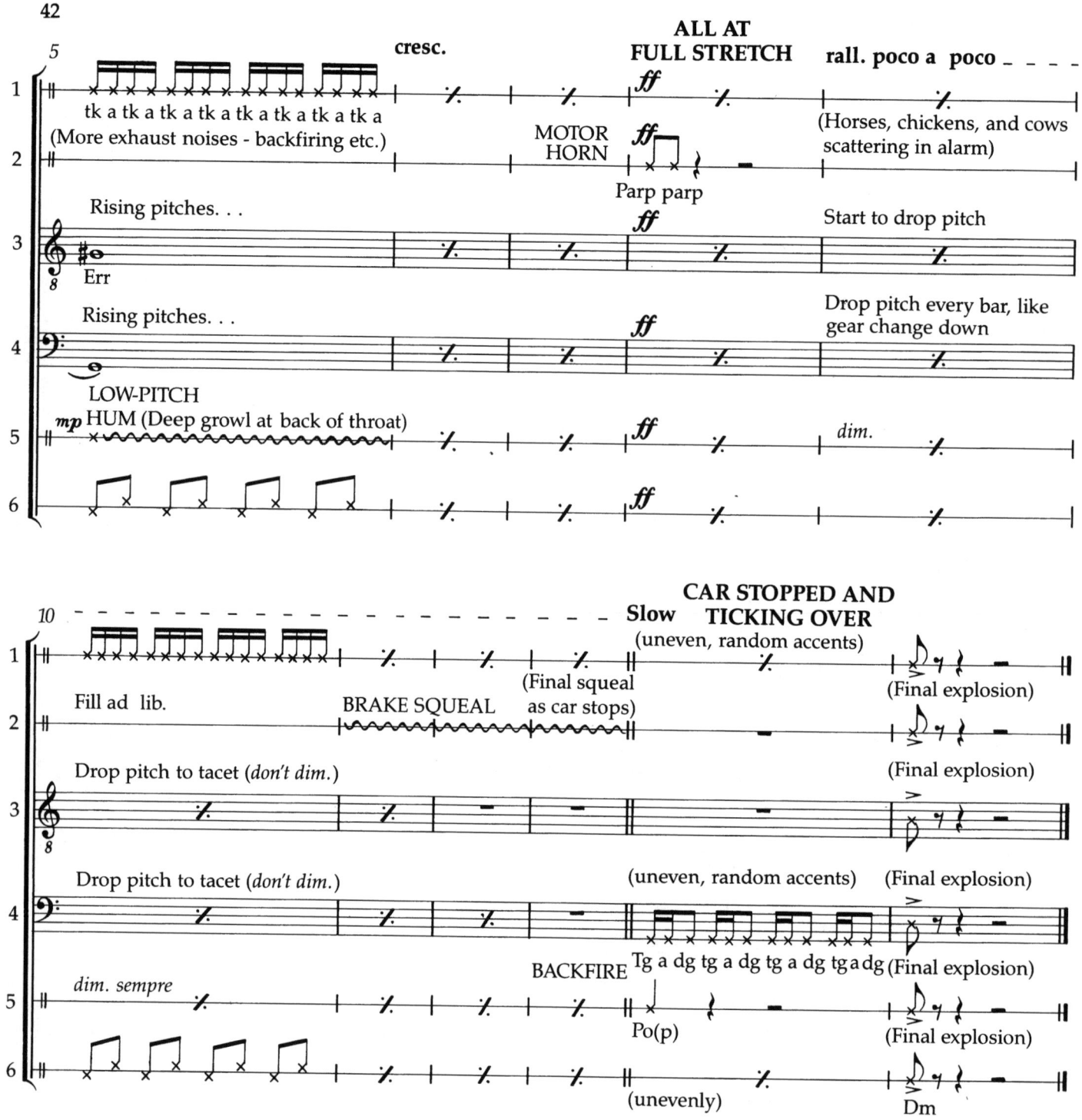

NARRATOR:

Sure enough, it was Toad; he jumped down from his car.

'I say, you chaps,' he said, 'what do you think of her? Straight eight, with sleeve valves of course . . . family crest on the door . . . does nearly fifty downhill!'

Badger interrupted sternly. 'Toad, you unhappy creature!'

'Me unhappy?' exclaimed Toad; 'What a lot of rot you do talk, Badger. Why, I'm the happiest creature alive! The open road . . . the smell of hot oil . . . if you chaps can't recognize the coming thing when you see it, then I'm afraid progress won't wait for you, and no more shall I . . . Must be off! See you all up at my place some time.'

And with that, Toad started up the car again and drove off. But that wasn't the end of it, as I'm afraid we shall see . . .

8: COURT SCENE

(Usher, Magistrate, Toad)

USHER: Silence! Silence in court!

* MAGISTRATE: Never in all my time as a magistrate. . . never in all the long years I've served on this bench. . . never has been seen a creature more abjectly despicable, a Toad more steeped in the molasses of criminality, more tarred with the glue of felonious

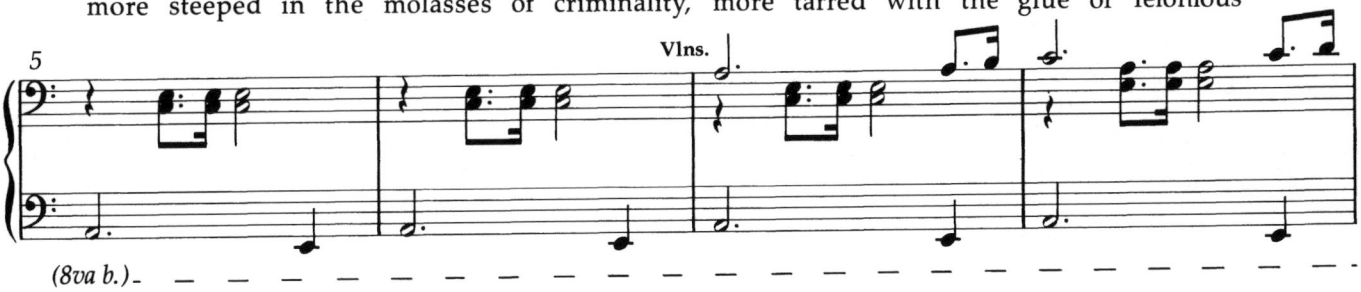

turpitude than the hardened criminal we see melting like a fly-blown marshmallow before our averted eyes. Pull yourself together, prisoner! Be a man, and prepare to hear your

sentence! You shall be taken from this place and be flung into the deepest, darkest, and most vile-smelling dungeon that the resources of the County Gaol can provide. And there

* During the delivery of the Magistrate's speech, TOAD utters appropriate wails, groans, etc.

you shall languish, on the first count—stealing a motor car—ten years; on the second count—driving in a most reckless and dangerous manner—fifteen years; on the

third count—insulting a policeman—twenty years. And in view of the seriousness of the offences and the hardened criminality of the felon, I order that these terms

of imprisonment be served both consecutively and concurrently. . . Take him away!*

* Speech and music should finish at approximately the same time.

NARRATOR:

Toad, abject and downcast, was led away roughly by two horny-handed gaolers and thrown into the nastiest of dungeons, with nothing for company save the occasional spider, and no solace save that provided by a tin mug of brackish water and the stale crusts thrown to him from time to time . . . and, oh, I nearly forgot – the rather comely and kind-hearted daughter of one of the gaolers. Let us eavesdrop as she attempts to rally the starving and disconsolate felon . . .

9: IN PRISON

(Toad and Gaoler's Daughter)

10
Li-ver 'n lights?
Fish is good for the brain, they say;
TOAD
(faint)
Well . . .
p
13
Like some bloa-ters in brine?
Don't you fan - cy things
parlando
Some o-ther time . . .
mp
p
(Makes hand - to - mouth "oops" gesture)
16
sal - ty then?
Well, toad - in-the - hole tastes
simp - ly di - vine!
(TOAD looks horrified)

A
19
f enthusiastically
Kid-neys is nice all swim-ming in grease:
Don't you fan - cy a few?
mf
mp
22
mf temptingly again
Want to try some-thing new?
Well there's cold
faint and weak
I don't think I do . . .
relieved
Phew!
p
mf
p
25
cresc.
jel-lied eel with a nice sli-my feel!
f triumphant
Pig's trot - ter and sheep's
mf
gliss.
3

28
head stew
Tastes all jui - cy and fine;
fainter and weaker
I can just i - ma - gine . . .
p
31
Wash it down with a glass or two . . .
p conspiratorial
Of me home-made
hopeful at last
Oo!
f
mf
p
34
B
f
crab - ap - ple wine!
Sweet - breads and kip - pers with spi - nach for veg.
Ugh!
B
f

37
mp cresc.
Takes your ap - pe - tite ov - er the edge. Stewed mut - ton and
f
p cresc.
40
f brazen
dump - lin's then, Just walk up and help your-self a -
f
42
p coyly
- gain and a - gain: I bet you I got a few treats you nev - er
p

NARRATOR:

Nothing the gaoler's daughter had to offer seemed to rouse him. But like all great men of history, his single-mindedness saw him through. He escaped by exchanging clothes with a humble washerwoman; let us join him as he makes his way back to Toad Hall, a sadder and a wiser Toad . . . (*Narration continues over start of No. 10*)

10: ON THE ROAD TO TOAD HALL

(Toad and Chorus)

NARRATOR:. . . I'm not sure that's true, actually, but perhaps I'd better let you be the judge; here he is.

Bright, breezy and fast-moving (♩=144)

12
I've got chic, I've got cha-ris-ma, I've got mys-tique;
15
All my friends tell me so, And af-ter all, they ought to know.
p
19
Such an air de-bon-air! Such so-phis-ti-ca-ted
22
sa-voir-faire! So dé-ga-gé, so é-lite, The

25
CHORUS
A
S.
mf
A.
Oo
T.
B.
mf
f
peo - ple come and cheer me when I walk down the street. I'm the Toad, I'm the
A
f
28
mp
mf
the great - est! Oo It's the lat - est!
mp
mf
great - est! I set the style;

31
p
mp
f
Oo
tell you how
Ssh!
p
mp
f
So stay a - while
and
I'll tell you how
p
In the
mf
34
mf
strict - est con - fi - dence
I get called
by Scot - land Yard;
They
mf
37
3
f
have to bring me in when a case gets too hard.
Ein - stein took

40
CHORUS
f
Eu - re - ka!
f
(TOAD)
mf
les - sons from me; I showed him that m c squared e-quals e;
mp
43
p dolce
Ah
p dolce
Doo doo doo
mf
3
Mo - zart and Schu - bert and Lud - wig van B. Would have
p

45
doo
Doo doo doo doo
Ah
had a lot more hits if they had stu - died with me!
mf
47
Mi - chel - an - ge-lo's draw - ing was ab - so - lute - ly ap - pal - ling; If
p

49
B
f
Toad
f
f
Toad had done the Sis - tine cei - ling You would find it more ap - peal - ing. Toad is the
B
f
52
mp
mf
You said it! Oo It oc - curred to us.
mp
mf
mf
great - est! Ge - ni - us is real - ly the word . . . A
mf

55
mp
mf
f
Oo at the Pa - lace Well!
mp
mf
f
knight-hood should be con - ferred on Toad. O. K.,
f
p
58
C
mf
wa wa doo wa
mf
Doo be doo be doo wa
f
make it a peer - age! So I hope you get the mes-sage loud and clear: If you
C
f

61
wa wa doo wa doo be
Doo be doo be doo wa
can't re-solve a prob-lem, why, just bring it here. Pluck up cou-rage,
64
doo be doo be doo wa
don't be shy; Ga-li-le-o made the big time 'cos he gave me a try! When

67
mf
wa wa doo wa wa wa
mf
Doo be doo be doo wa Doo be doo
New-ton saw that ap-ple drop from the tree, Well, he asked me what it meant, And I
mf
70
f
mp
Wow! Oo
f
mp
mf
That's gra-vi-ty!
said: Sci-ence and in-ven-tion are most-ly due To Pro-
f
mp

73
D
f
Who? Toad is the
mf
He's too good to be true!
f
- fes - sor Toad.
Toad is the
D
f
76
p
great - est; We know it; So let's get the show on the road, And sa -
p
great - est!
p

79
cresc.
f
- lute the phe-no - me-nal, the fa - bu-lous, fan-tas - tic,
cresc.
f
f
cresc.
Sen - sa - tio-nal, suc-cess-ful, scin -
p cresc.
f cresc.
82
(senza rit.)
ff
Toad!
Yeah!
Segue No. 11
ff
ff
- til - la - ting su - per - star Toad!
(senza rit.)
Segue No. 11
ff

11: THE PLAN

(Mole, Toad, Rat, Badger)

10
Rat! Hal-lo, Mole! Why don't you all come down to my place for a spot of
13
lun-cheon?
BADGER
f
Luck-less Toad!
slow and solemn
You no lon - ger have a place!
colla voce
ff
B
16
MOLE
f
. . . the wea - sels! . . . the
TOAD
f
. . . the wea - sels! . . . the
RAT
f
. . . the wea - sels! . . . the
While you were in prison,
Toad Hall was invaded by the wea - sels . . . the fer - rets . . .
B
colla voce
trem.
p
cresc.
Ped.
Ped.

20 MOLE
fer - rets . . .
. . . and the stoats!
TOAD
fer - rets . . .
. . . and the stoats!
ff
O
RAT
fer - rets . . .
. . . and the stoats!
BADGER
. . . and the stoats!
f
23 TOAD
hor - ror!
Ca - tas - tro - phe ap - pal - ling!
ff
f
26
mf freely
O mi - se - ry! O in - jus - tice! Now I'm ru - ined!
C
Slow (♩ = 60)
A - lack!
mp
p

29
MOLE
TOAD
RAT
BADGER
mf
f freely
Allegro vivace (♩ =144)
Now listen to me, Toad: all is not lost, undeserving though you are . . .
I have a plan.
colla voce
colla voce
Allegro vivace (♩ =144)
f
33
D
f
. . . with knives!
f
. . . with knives!
f
. . . with knives!
mf
We must arm our-selves with knives . . .
with
D
trem.
trem. sempre
sf
p

36
. . . with cud-gels!
. . . with cud-gels!
. . . with cud-gels!
cud-gels. . .
. . . and with pis-tols of a-larm - ing as-pect;
f
39
colla voce
f
A-ha!
f
A-ha!
f
A-ha!
p
. . . gain entry to Toad Hall by a secret tunnel, the presence of which was fortunately made known to me by Toad's august father many long years ago. . .
. . . then we ad -
colla voce
p

68
E
accel.
42
cresc. sempre
f
-vance up - on the wea - sels and the fer - rets and the stoats, bran - dish - ing our wea - pons and
E
accel.
p
cresc.
freely (recit.)
In tempo (♩ = c. 112)
45
MOLE
p timidly
A fe - ro - cious and blood - cur - dling
TOAD
p timidly
A fe - ro - cious and blood - cur - dling
RAT
p timidly
A fe - ro - cious and blood - cur - dling
(BADGER)
freely (recit.)
sing - ing a fe - ro - cious and blood - cur - dling cho - rus.
freely (recit.)
In tempo (♩ = c. 112)
f
f
p

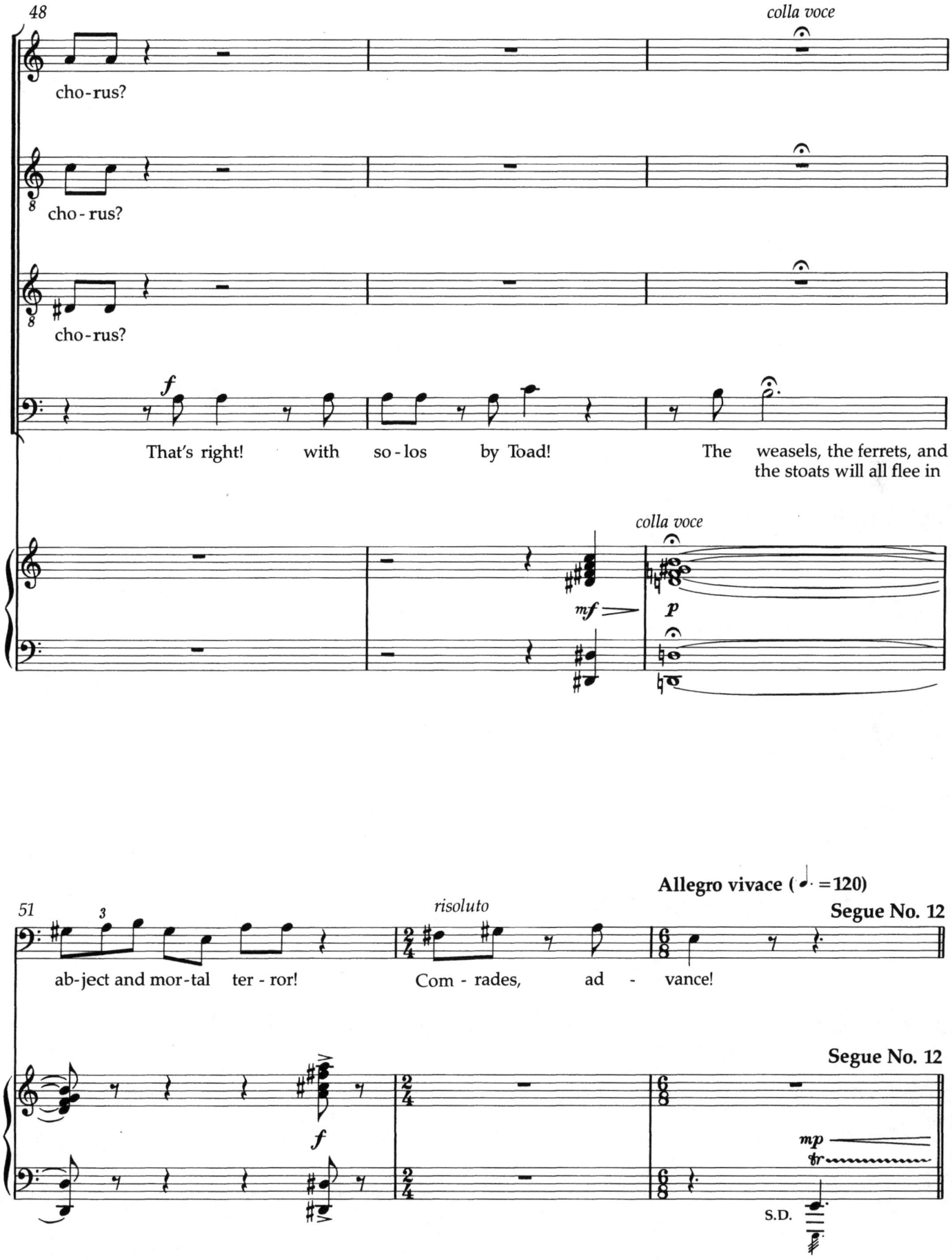
48
colla voce
cho-rus?
cho-rus?
cho-rus?
f
That's right! with so-los by Toad! The weasels, the ferrets, and the stoats will all flee in
colla voce
mf
p
51
3
risoluto
Allegro vivace (♩. = 120)
Segue No. 12
ab-ject and mor-tal ter-ror! Com-rades, ad-vance!
Segue No. 12
f
mp
tr
S.D.

12: RECAPTURE OF TOAD HALL (Let's wallop a weasel)

(Mole, Toad, Rat, Badger)

16
f MOLE
Toad Hall is Toad's hall— Let's go ov - er the top!
f TOAD
Toad Hall is Toad's hall— Let's go ov - er the top!
f RAT
Toad Hall is Toad's hall— Let's go ov - er the top!
f BADGER
Toad Hall is Toad's hall— Let's go ov - er the top!
dim.
20
A
p
Tip - toe up the stair - case . . . Tip - toe
pp
Tip - toe
pp
Tip - toe
pp
Tip - toe
pp
Tip - toe
A
p
pp

* In this number, the shrieks and cries of the weasels, ferrets, and stoats are to be allocated to suitable members of the chorus.

32
mf
Lay them neat - ly out in pairs,
f
Lis - ten while they
un - a - wares,
cresc.
mf
36
f
Let's go ov - er the top!
say their prayers, Let's go ov - er the top!
Let's go ov - er the top!
Let's go ov - er the top!
f
(f)
dim.

74
B
(MOLE, TOAD RAT, and BADGER)
40
f
Pin 'em up by the ears, chaps, Spear 'em down to the floor!
mf
44
Wea - sel - bur - ger and chips is a treat that we a - dore!
48
RAT
mp
Shred the stoats in lit - tle bits,
TOAD
mf
Let's have a fer - ret chop!
MOLE, TOAD, RAT, and BADGER
f
It's
p cresc.
f
52
(Smack lips)
wea - sel-whack-in' good,
So let's go ov - er the

56
MOLE
accel.
C Più mosso (♩.=144)
top!
Watch it, there goes a wea - sel!
TOAD
top! Thwack thwack thwack thwack thwack thwack thwack
RAT
top! Thwack thwack thwack thwack thwack thwack thwack
BADGER
top! Thwack thwack thwack thwack thwack thwack thwack
accel.
C Più mosso (♩.=144)
60
WEASEL
MOLE
Thwack, thwack, splat! (Groan) Swish swish swish Got him!
thwack thwack splat! Strike him! yes, it's a stoat! Got him!
thwack thwack splat! Swish swish swish Got him!
thwack thwack splat! Swish swish swish Got him!
64
FERRET and STOAT
MOLE
Squashed him flat! Eergh! Buc-kle buc-kle
Squashed him flat! Buc-kle buc-kle
Squashed him flat! Fer - ret by the door there, He'd
Squashed him flat! Swash swash

68
MOLE
buc - kle swash, Yes, Toad Hall is Toad's hall;
TOAD
buc - kle swash, Yes, Toad Hall is Toad's hall;
RAT
look more peace - ful dead! Toad Hall is Toad's hall;
BADGER
swash swash, Yes, Toad Hall is Toad's hall;
72
Have we ta - ken care of them all? Ah
Have we ta - ken care of them all? Ah
Have we ta - ken care of them all? Ah
Have we ta - ken care of them all? Search be - hind the gar - den wall?

13: NARRATION

NARRATOR:

Every last weasel, ferret and stoat fled in panic and disorder, and Toad Hall was once more Toad's. Badger lectured Toad sternly, reminding him that his folly and boastfulness had nearly cost him his liberty and his home, and Toad promised to mend his ways.

The next night a celebration banquet was held at Toad Hall, and everyone made merry. It was nearly midnight when Badger rose to his feet, rather unsteadily, and addressed the assembled company. (*Attacca No. 14*)

14: FINALE

(TOAD, BADGER, and CHORUS)

7
. . . the fer - rets, . . .
and the stoats,
fer - rets . . .
and the stoats . . .
has
Ped.
calmando
A Tempo I (♩ = 104)
11
sostenuto
fi - nal - ly been re - stored to its right - ful ow - ner.
I give you the toast:
legato
mp
14 CHORUS
S.
mf dolce
p
A.
Hearth
and
home!
T.
B.
mf dolce
p
Hearth
and
home!
mf
p

18
colla voce
ff
Hear, hear!
ff
BADGER
And now I call upon our good friend, Mr Toad,
to make a brief re - ply.
colla voce
p
B
(♩ =104 sempre)
21
TOAD
quiet and thoughtful
p legato sempre
I could ne - ver have come back
If it had - n't been for you, my friends;
p
sim.
25
A house can seem emp - ty,
so you wan - der,
And you think you've no friends . . .

29 stringendo
(♩=132)
cresc.
mf
There are so ma - ny things that I ne - ver real - ly saw be - fore,
cresc.
mf
C
33 rall. poco a poco
Slow and calm (♩=72)
mp
dim.
But I think that I can see them clear - ly now:
dim.
p
(+Hp. 8ve)
Fl.
con Ped.
37
p
musing
The ket - tle on the hob, The chest - nuts in the fire, The
40
rit.
slip - pers by the rock - ing chair And wood - smoke drift - ing through the air. . . I
Ped.

43
moving on faster
think that per-haps . . . It's time that per-haps . . . I star - ted, per-haps, To
Ped.
Ped.
Ped.
46
rit.
(a tempo)
D Moderato (♩=96)
think a-bout set - tl -ing down.
pp
p
con Ped.
50
CHORUS
ALL VOICES
p dolce e legato
Home is a spe - cial kind of feel - ing:
54
The feel - ing of a place where you be - long;

58
poco cresc.
mp
A feel - ing that the world is left be - hind you,
poco cresc.
mp
poco cresc.
mp
62
unis.
Like a shel - ter from your care That seems to want you to be
E
66
Home is that spe - cial kind of feel - ing:
S.
mp
(A.T.B.) (Hum)
T.
B.
there.
E

70
The feel - ing that you've made it all your own;
(hum)
74
(mp)
mf
place,
Some-where which you know is real - ly your place,
mp
mf
mf
78
A place for liv - ing;
mp
p
(A.
T.
B.)
(Hum)
Your spe - cial place, your home.
mp
p
mp
p

82
F
mf warmly
Home has a
mf warmly
F
mf warmly
86
wel - come kind of feel - ing: The fire - light and the
90
mp
warmth of hearth and home;
(S. A.) (Hum)
A wel - come that you
mf
(B.) mp Hum
mp

94
Like a
mp
know will al - ways cheer you,
97
gen - tle fond 'hel - lo' that seems to touch you with a
A.
T.
B.
(Hum)
mp
(Hum)
100
glow.
G
mf
Home has a qui - et kind of
G
mf
7
mf

103
feel - ing: An is - land when you
106
need to be a - lone; A ha - ven for the
mp
mp
mp
110
mf
mp
p
There's no - where bet - ter,
times you spend to - ge - ther;
A.
T.
B.
(Hum)
No
mf
mp
p
mf
mp
p

NARRATOR: Mole caught Rat's eye; Rat's eye caught Badger's eye. Each knew what home meant to the other. Nobody managed to catch Toad's

eye, but then Toad's eye was roving and resting lovingly an every detail of his home; worth a thousand gipsy caravans, worth a million motor cars, thought Toad.